W9-CKL-949

OFFICIAL BIRDSEYE VIEW—WORLD'S COLUMBIAN EXPOSITION, CHICAGO, 1893.

Chicago from the Air

THEN AND NOW

Chicago from the Air

THEN AND NOW

Thomas J. O'Gorman

THUNDER BAY
P·R·E·S·S

San Diego, California

Thunder Bay Press
An imprint of the Baker & Taylor Publishing Group
10350 Barnes Canyon Road, San Diego, CA 92121
www.thunderbaybooks.com

Produced by Salamander Books,
an imprint of Anova Books Ltd.
10 Southcombe Street, London W14 0RA, UK

"Then and Now" is a registered trademark of Anova Books Ltd.

© 2010 Salamander Books

Copyright under International, Pan American, and Universal Copyright Conventions.
All rights reserved. No part of this book may be reproduced or transmitted in any form
or by any means, electronic or mechanical, including photocopying, recording, or by any
information storage-and-retrieval system, without written permission from the copyright
holder. Brief passages (not to exceed 1,000 words) may be quoted for reviews.

"Thunder Bay" is a registered trademark of Baker & Taylor. All rights reserved.

All notations of errors or omissions should be addressed to Thunder Bay Press,
Editorial Department, at the above address. All other correspondence (author
inquiries, permissions) concerning the content of this book should be addressed
to Salamander Books, 10 Southcombe Street, London W14 0RA, UK.

ISBN-13: 978-1-60710-009-6
ISBN-10: 1-60710-009-6

Library of Congress Cataloging-in-Publication Data available upon request.

1 2 3 4 5 14 13 12 11 10

Printed in China

DEDICATION
In memory of Gordon St. George Mark

ACKNOWLEDGMENTS
I would like to thank the people who have helped me research and write this book: Gary Johnson,
President, Chicago History Museum. Rob Medina, Rights and Reproduction Coordinator, Photo
Duplication Department, Chicago History Museum. Tim Samuelson, Cultural Historian,
Department of Cultural Affairs, City of Chicago. Honorable Edward M. Burke, Chairman, Chicago
City Council, Committee on Finance. Maxwell Mueller, City of Chicago. Honorable James J.
McDonough, McDonough & Associates, Chicago.

PICTURE CREDITS
The publisher wishes to thank the following for kindly supplying the photographs that appear in
this book:

"Then" photographs:
All "Then" images in the book were supplied courtesy of Corbis images with the exception of the
following:
Chicago History Museum: pages 22, ICHi-13657; 24, ICHi-05828; 26, ICHi-04091; 28, ICHi-61584;
38, ICHi-00948; 44, ICHi-61583; 48, ICHi-29269; 50, ICHi-05776; 76, ICHi-34304; 88, ICHi-05805;
118, ICHi-23565; 120, ICHi-26912; 122, ICHi-01513; 124, ICHi-05789; 128, ICHi-05765; 130, ICHi-
23523; 138, ICHi-05790.
Getty Images: pages 10, 42, 43 (inset), 96, 102 (Margaret Bourke-White), 116 (main), 136.
Library of Congress: pages 16, HAER ILL, 16-CHIG, 138-11; 18, LC-USZ62-41402; 46, HABS ILL,
16-CHIG, 110A-83; 52, HAER ILL, 16-CHIG, 154-3; 70, LC-USZ62-123211; 84, LC-DIG-ppmsca-
18100; 98, LC-USZ62-126620; 104, LC-USZC4-1835; 140, LC-USZ62-53414.
University of Chicago: page 32, apf2-02581.

"Now" photographs:
All "Now" images were taken by Karl Mondon with the exception of the following:
Alamy: page 115
Corbis: page 72 (inset)
Getty Images: page 75 (inset)
Kelly Hafermann: pages 105 and 117 (inset)

Endpapers show: Bird's-eye view of Chicago before the Great Chicago Fire of 1871 (Corbis); bird's-
eye view of the 1893 World's Fair (Library of Congress, LC-USZC4-1570). The map on page 142 is
reproduced courtesy of Chicago Office of Tourism.

Anova Books is committed to respecting the intellectual property rights of others. We have
therefore taken all reasonable efforts to ensure that the reproduction of all content on these
pages is done with the full consent of copyright owners. If you are aware of any unintentional
omissions, please contact the company directly so that any necessary corrections may be made
for future editions.

Introduction

Chicago's spacious lakefront provides one of America's largest cities with something few other American cities possess—an elegant, pristine coastline. This is no *On the Waterfront* geography like Hoboken in New Jersey or Marseilles in France. Chicago's twenty-eight-mile-long lake parkland is more similar to Rio's Ipanema, Copacabana, or Corcovado hugging the everyday life of local citizens (just not in the subzero temperatures of winter). It is hard to imagine as you walk through the sand that three and a half million people live just west of Lake Shore Drive. This is why Chicagoans stroll and promenade, run and bike, swim and float along its edge. Sailboats with spinnakers full fly under heavy lake wind from spring through fall. Then winter sets in.

"Then and Now" is an intriguing concept, permitting the reader/viewer the opportunity to become immersed in the sweeping eras of immense urban change in Chicago. I see this work as a companion to Elizabeth McNulty's earlier title *Chicago Then and Now*. We have worked hard to expand this view and to avoid overlapping. But while Elizabeth's book shows how much of Chicago's elegant past has been preserved, this book vividly illustrates many of the huge changes that are so easily observed from an aerial viewpoint.

As a Chicagoan I am pleased with the natural flow of the geographical layout of this work—from south to north—across the cityscape from the curving border with Indiana to leafy Evanston with its elegant "town and gown" character. It is a good way in which to come to know this noble metropolis, seen from the sky and sometimes from the roadway too. We have been generous to include many stunning ground shots along the way, hoping to quell any vertigo readers might experience when viewing the lofty panoramas from the clouds, then or now.

There are places in America where change might mean a different color of paint or a new carpet on the floor. But as Chicago has shown, it might mean reversing the flow of the river (1900), splitting the atom under the football stands of the University of Chicago (1942), or creating an urban mountain range out of glass and steel-framed buildings (1890 to the present). In Chicago this kind of change has become commonplace.

Many of these powerful changes in Chicago are easy to see, thanks to our then and now photo comparisons. Sometimes it is hard to judge what is a more grandiose change—the creation of the first concrete expressway (the Eisenhower in 1954) that still races along the flatland of the prairie, neighborhood after neighborhood; or the shifting of the path of the Chicago River a quarter of a mile to the west (1928); or the creation of America's most spectacular urban promenade, Millennium Park (2004), financed through corporate giving rather than taxpayer dollars, on what for decades was old railroad land.

Buildings are tall in Chicago, but size is relative. Chicago is not some oil-rich kingdom of new money. We do not look for height, but instead look for elegance of design. Though many buildings now tower over the shimmering white terra-cotta Wrigley Building, it remains the favorite of Chicagoans.

This book catalogs change that is tactile and visible from the air and on the ground—across Chicago's streetscapes, back alleys, front lawns, museums, and professional sports stadia. At present there is another "flow reversal" underway—the turning around of the urban flight of the past century as empty-nesters return to the heart of the city seeking the richness of Chicago's urban life. Suburban manses are exchanged for downtown condos, where access to art, theater, restaurants, and prime shopping is available without the necessity of an automobile. This is a massive social change and it recalibrates how people live in a great city. You do not have to fight to survive in this metropolis—it is easy to live well.

It used to be said among Fortune 500 companies that the most difficult thing to get young executives to agree to was to move to Chicago. Now it is said that the most difficult thing to do is to get them to move from Chicago. What changed was peoples' experience of the livability of Chicago—small-town customs and big-city demeanor. Here is first-rate opera (the Lyric), award-winning music (the Chicago Symphony), engaging sports rivalries (the Cubs and the White Sox), and the largest collection of French Impressionists and Postimpressionists outside of the Musée d'Orsay in Paris.

The streets are thick with great restaurants—from the five-star variety to hole-in-the-wall Italian of Tuscan, Neapolitan, Milanese, and Sicilian styles, thanks to the waves of Mediterranean folk who came here. But that is not to exclude very popular Mexican, Thai, and Vietnamese styles, newer to Chicago palettes as well. Of course there are the traditional Chicago steak restaurants where large slabs of beef are the common fare, a reminder of the city's roots in the meatpacking days of the past. The stockyards may be long gone, but Chicagoans' passion for large cuts of rib eye persists.

But it is not just food that has altered life here, it is also schools. Over the past decade the city has reinvented its public school system, good news for any family moving to the city. That move remains the talk of the nation and is a critical component to everyday life.

Chicago is greener, more cosmopolitan, and more ethnically diverse than ever. The parkland boulevards are broad and ingeniously connect to one another right across the city in a network of early urban planning. And as the winter ends, as if by magic every March 17, the Chicago River turns a brilliant emerald green, injecting new life into a city waking from its winter slumber.

CHICAGO: A HISTORY

Below: *The charred remains of a great city sit in neat piles along the riverfront. Small shanties were quickly constructed out of the remaining usable timber. The tall ships have curiously returned to the river that was once home to warehouses and grain silos. It is hard to imagine that the great architectural muscle of buildings like the Merchandise Mart would rise up from these cinders.*

"PRINCE, THE BOYS"

On September 21, 1860, Edward Albert—the Prince of Wales and son of Queen Victoria—stopped in Chicago on his return home from Canada. His arrival in Chicago stirred a great deal of commotion. It is said that 50,000 people lined the streets to see him pass—half the population of the city at that time. On his schedule was a stop at Chicago's city hall, where he was to meet the members of the Chicago City Council. The task of introducing him fell to the mayor, "Long John" Wentworth. When the prince entered the council, the mayor's remarks were short and sweet: "Prince, the boys," he said, then added, "Boys, the Prince!" His words are worth remembering because in them is contained the brassy, succinct, uncluttered efficiency that has always made Chicago what it is. Chicago had incorporated as a town only twenty-seven years before the arrival of the prince. And it had been a city for only twenty-three years. Already it was the fastest-growing city on the planet. What was the secret of such rapid growth in the heartland of the nation? Location! Location! Location!

THE PLACE THAT SMELLS LIKE ONIONS

Here along the waters of the great Lake Michigan—long the home of the Potawatomi, the Miami, and the Ottawa Indians—waves of new settlers arrived. It was the Native American people who first coined what would be the city's name—Chi-ca-goua—meaning "the place that smells like onions," because of the heavy odor wafting across the prairie from the wild onion, *Allium tricoccum*.

Early in the nineteenth century, an engineer serving in the U.S. army, Captain John Whistler (grandfather of the painter James McNeill Whistler), supervised the construction of Fort Dearborn, the farthest point west for the infant American republic. The stockade outpost, named to honor Secretary-of-War Henry Dearborn, was to guard the gateway to "no man's land"—as the land beyond the fort was known—the pathways followed by the fur trappers and the traders who roamed the interior of the wilderness. In 1812, however, what would later become Chicago faced its first great disaster: the Fort Dearborn massacre. Indians, allied with the British during the War of 1812, caught up with the soldiers and settlers trying to get to Fort Detroit, along the shore of the lakefront at what is today Nineteenth Street, and slaughtered them all. They then burned the fort.

FIRST, A CANAL

Within fifty years of the 1803 construction of the fort, a canal joined Lake Michigan to the Illinois River ninety miles away. If you sailed through what was known as the Illinois and Michigan Canal, the next stop was the Gulf of Mexico, through New Orleans, by way of the Mississippi River. That meant that all water traffic in the nation's interior had one essential place to pass through to reach those commercial markets—Chicago.

NEXT, THE RAILROAD

Within fifty years, the railroad began to change the way the nation moved people and commerce. Whether you traveled east or west, north or south, soon there was only one place through which all the trains must pass—again, Chicago. All of this came about not exclusively by Mother Nature; much of it had to do with the intricacies of local politics in which the muscle of Chicago's Washington politicos—like Senator Stephen A. Douglas—were essential in bringing the best deals back home. As the hub of the nation's transport system, Chicago's future fortune was made.

Nothing did that more than the marriage of the livestock industry, centered at the Union Stock Yards, and the railroads, with some help from the invention of refrigeration. With that the meatpacking industry, at one time Chicago's most essential business, was born. Livestock, killed and dressed in Chicago, found its way as fresh meat on the platters of America and beyond. And the massive proportions of this growing industry were ripe for the arrival of another massive wave of new Chicagoans—European immigrants ready for work.

THE GREAT FIRE AND THE DRIVE OF INDUSTRY

On October 8, 1871, the Great Chicago Fire destroyed almost four square miles of the city. The raging inferno caused $200 million in damage and left a third of the city's inhabitants without a home. But it was Chicago's swift recovery from this incredible setback that shocked her detractors—within two years the entire city was rebuilt. It is no accident that Chicago made such a remarkable recovery, as the city was filled with people of bold ideas and a willingness to work. Great fortunes had been made in industries related to the railroad, like George Pullman's success creating the railroad sleeping car. Meatpacking was like a license to print money for families like the Armours, the Swifts, and the Morrises—titans of the industry. There were also the department store barons, Marshall Field and Levi Leiter; the Ryerson steel princes; and the imperial McCormicks, whose grandfather invented the "reaper"—an agricultural harvesting machine.

More fortunes were yet to come in chewing gum, newspaper publishing, and hotels.

WAVES OF NEW IMMIGRANTS

Every ten years the population of Chicago doubled so that by 1890 there were a million people living in the city, a large portion of them still learning English. By 1900 there were 1.6 million residents. Assimilation became the new and indispensable goal—becoming American came easy after becoming a Chicagoan. Once the language could be mastered, the job market opened up to larger opportunities than the slaughter of livestock or peddling door-to-door. The massive numbers of Irish arrived, carrying that most indispensable of tools: the full use of the English language. Without the need to wait a generation, they were soon

Below: *The largest commercial building in the world—the Merchandise Mart, with twenty-five floors—may not have height, but it has a girth that spans two city blocks. It was the Art Deco dream of Marshall Field in the late 1920s, and it opened the gates for nonstop wholesale shopping in interior and exterior design.*

Right: *Chicago's railroad past is deeply etched in the earth in this photo. Tracks, now long gone, surround the Grant Park framework, modest then in its design. Tracks reach all the way to the river on what stood for decades as derelict land. The breakwater along the right demonstrates the passion for creating safe harbors—all man-made—pointing to the quirky relationship between the Chicago residents and the lake. At the center is the river's mouth—the gateway to the interior of North America—and the white tower of the Wrigley Building.*

employed as police officers, firefighters, and translators, helping to broker deals for those who did not have the everyday use of English—like their German, Polish, and Lithuanian neighbors. Soon, the Irish parlayed their knack for being good neighbors into elected public service careers. By the end of the nineteenth century—out of this remarkable confluence of public service, governmental leadership, and political shenanigans—the coin of the realm in Chicago became the art of political governance. The Irish knew this—and they were good at it. All of this pushed Chicago toward fresh change and remarkable urban growth.

THE CHICAGO WORLD'S FAIR

The World's Columbian Exposition of 1893—commonly known as the Chicago World's Fair—marked a profound moment of change in Chicago life. Of course, it was supposed to celebrate the anniversary of the arrival of Christopher Columbus in the New World four centuries earlier. In fact, what it really celebrated was Chicago's miraculous recovery from the flames, and its success rising bigger, stronger, more refined, and more modern than any other city on earth. A big boast, but few people argued about that after they saw their first telephone, phonograph, electric lightbulb, combine harvester, or the electric elevated trains running along tracks above the city streets. Equally impressive were the Home Insurance Building, the very first skyscraper, designed by William Le Baron Jenney and standing ten stories—and the eighteen-story tower of the Auditorium Building on Michigan Avenue that Dankmar Adler and Louis Sullivan had designed. Adler and Sullivan's building—an opera house, hotel, and offices all rolled into one—was then the tallest building in the nation. All of this captured the attention of the city's 27 million visitors, including the infanta of Spain, who caught a glimpse of the world to come.

A LOOK INTO THE FUTURE

The future of Chicago would bring about some curious incidents. Imagine what people must have thought when Mrs. Potter Palmer unveiled her vast collection of French Impressionist paintings at the fair with her art all out of focus and off-kilter. Or what the farmers from Iowa and the Dakotas thought while riding around on Mr. George Ferris's large iron wheel at fifty cents a spin. Or what the vast numbers of small-town American families thought when they saw their first Cairo Street, or Irish Village, or Daniel Burnham's neoclassical White City along the avenues of the exposition. The modern world had arrived and it was here to stay, especially in Chicago. Within fifty years of the close of the fair, not far from the Midway amusement park, scientists at the University of Chicago split the atom for the very first time.

PIONEERING ARCHITECTURE

Something powerful had been set in motion by the grandeur of the 1893 fair. Even on the dusty prairie a new sophistication was in the air. The powerful economy made a new kind of American royalty appear—the barons of vast prairie fortunes. In Chicago, many had learned the important life lesson that made generosity a part of local character. A public responsibility to the city that had made them rich became an important construct of everyday life. The wonders engendered by such philanthropy still fill the streets and public places of Chicago life—the museums, the symphony orchestra, and the opera.

Because Chicago had a tradition for remarkable architecture, it is reasonable to assume that such a tradition would continue to thrive. And it did. It is no accident that the nation's first steel-framed glass skyscraper was developed in Chicago in 1894—Daniel Burnham and John Wellborn Root's fourteen-story Reliance Building at the corner of State and Washington streets. This is the mother of all steel-framed glass buildings. It was not long before significant architecture became an ordinary part of everyday life.

Frank Lloyd Wright was a young man, wandering throughout Chicago and surviving on bananas, when he took himself to the door of architects Dankmar Adler and Louis Sullivan to ask for employment. He got the job. Perhaps nothing has had such a dynamic, transformative effect on Chicago than the stunning array of architects who made Chicago home in every generation. The legacy of their artistry lives on in libraries, cathedrals, department stores, family homes, high-rise apartments, office buildings, as well as in an impressive array of government buildings that lifted the city from one age to another. From humble beginnings at Old Fort Dearborn and Mark Beaubien's first primitive hotel on Wolf Point, the city now boasts the chic elevator of the John Hancock Center, the effusive swirl of the Wrigley Building, the mountainous rise of the Willis Tower, and the Grecian retro-classicism of Chicago's city hall.

Below: *The full sweep of the 1933 Century of Progress World's Fair, which unleashed visions of modern science, stands along the waters of the lakefront. The fair's continuity to the city's downtown presented fairgoers with a stunning taste of the future in the skyscrapers lining Grant Park. Overhead, the Sky-Ride carried visitors 219 feet above the ground in a rocket car. Outer space never seemed so close.*

Above: *Civil defense planes patrol the Chicago shorefront in May 1956, on station in case of an atomic attack. The postwar building boom is already in evidence downtown with the Wrigley Building now engulfed by its neighbors.*

But Chicago has battered neither the landscape nor the environment in its evolution as a great city, and it has not surrendered its passion for living by the water's edge.

THE EMERALD NECKLACE

The lakefront remains the "Emerald Necklace" of Daniel Burnham's dreams. The twenty-eight miles of pristine sandy beaches and parks remain well manicured and protected. No industry mars its beauty. To call Lake Michigan a "lake" does not do it justice; after all, you cannot see the other shore. More than 400 miles long and 100 miles wide, Lake Michigan is its own ecosystem, serving as the city's refrigerator in the summer and its heater in the winter. The lake changes minute by minute, inventing fresh colors.

THE CUBS VERSUS OPERA

But that does not mean that the lakefront is not used by countless Chicagoans for more than getting a tan or a swim. The lakefront is also Chicago's cradle of civilization, holding museums and grand institutions that honor science, industry, history, the sky, the sea, and even sports at Soldier Field, the Chicago Bears' football stadium.

The waterway is thick with harbors where sailboats anchor and large yachts moor. On one side of the city, North Siders are devoted to the Cubs and on the other, South Siders are loyal to the White Sox, demonstrating a fragmented sports dichotomy that outsiders cannot understand. In a curious clash of cultures, the two most difficult things to obtain in Chicago are tickets for a Cubs game or the Lyric Opera—both outrageous dramas.

Right: *Wrigley Field, home of the Chicago Cubs, is the anchor in this photo of the Lakeview neighborhood, affectionately known as "Wrigleyville." The neighborhood of lakeshore high-rises and typical Chicago six-flats is a unique piece of Chicago terrain with its own timeless history. A wide panorama looking south shows Navy Pier on the horizon.*

TALES OF THE RIVERBANK

But it is Chicago's "other" shoreline, the contouring, meandering waters of the Chicago River, just 156 miles long, that tells of the most pervasive change and transition in the city's history. The river's mouth was often filling with sand, making navigation difficult for ships. The U.S. Army Corps of Engineers came to dig out the mouth, so that the Illinois and Michigan Canal project could finish unimpeded. Between 1830 and 1833, the chief engineer on the project was a young Jefferson Davis, who would later become the president of the Confederate States of America. The completion of the canal, though, was nothing to the way in which Chicagoans greeted the dawn of the twentieth century—actually reversing the flow of the Chicago River, sending the detritus of millions down to St. Louis instead of into the city's water supply.

Powerful engineering projects have always had a grip on the imaginations of Chicago's leaders. Because of the river, Chicago is a city of bridges—thirty-six to be exact, more than any major city in the world. Some of Chicago's lifting-deck bascule bridges are more than a century old. They are themselves feats of architectural engineering both beautiful and functional; and since the 1996 Democratic National Convention, they are all painted a tasteful maroon.

THREE CENTURIES OF CHANGE

Europeans first saw Chicago in the seventeenth century when the adventurous French arrived, led by René-Robert Cavelier, Sieur de La Salle. Of course, this land belonged to France at the time. Remarkably, they saw something that stirred their souls—the impact of discovering that the powerful lake and the river were joined and had the ability to carry the courageous into the interior of the frontier. From that day forward, Chicago has never stopped changing, evolving, and transforming itself.

PANORAMIC MAP OF 1892

The Chicago lakefront is thick with sailboats and wooden merchant ships—part of the ebb and flow of its urban commerce. This image is set eight years before engineers reversed the flow of the Chicago River that ended nature's flow of the river into Lake Michigan—the source of Chicago's water supply. The open sewer of the river that moved the fumes of industrial and human waste was soon to be sent southward, out of harm's way for Chicagoans— much to the fury of its downstream neighbors. This bird's-eye view permits one to see the split of the Chicago River into its two branches. The vast expanse of the South Branch flowing on the left reaching all the way to the Gulf of Mexico via the Illinois and Michigan Canal to the Illinois River and onward to the Mississippi, finally reaches its mouth in New Orleans. On the right, the more modest North Branch wanders its way through the industrial corridor of the city out to the northern suburbs. Also clearly evident at the top of the frame is the vast expanse of the flatland of the prairie looking west at the horizon. Chicago was the gateway to the West, the hub of American transportation, and the meatpacking capital of the nation. Its ascendancy was the product of two essential commodities—its geographical location and the imaginative resourcefulness of its commercial barons. Through the mouth of the Chicago River, all the essential waterways of the heartland passed. It was the making of a great American city.

OVER A CENTURY OF CHANGE

Today the waters of the Chicago River still flow to the south from Lake Michigan. The silt that often clogged the mouth of the river is a problem of the past, as the mouth has been dug deep enough to permit easy passage. A system of locks now assists the passage of large ships, though most of the sail and rigging is from weekend sailors traveling along the lakeshore. The backdrop of urban life is now taller and more imaginative than ever, with three of the city's four tallest buildings in clear view. To the far left is the Aon Center (third-tallest) of white granite. On the right bank of the river is the Trump International Hotel and Tower (second-tallest and newest), and to the far right is the John Hancock Center (fourth-tallest overall but loftiest of the residential towers), with the Willis Tower (out of shot) remaining tallest of all. The expanse of city space demonstrates a fact of Chicago architecture—it is an evolving art. The world's first skyscraper, the Home Insurance Building by William Le Baron Jenney, was built in Chicago in 1885. Since then the form and function of architecture has guided Chicago's growth and has evolved into two Chicago schools of design, each of which has given it, and the world, the stunning wonder of glass and steel-frame construction. Scale, proportion, balance, and refinement of design have all helped to shape the grandeur of Chicago's own range of mountains on the flat ground of the prairie. Architecture is the coin of the realm in Chicago. After decades of neglect, the 525-acre Navy Pier (center foreground) was restored between 1976 and 1994.

SKYWAY BRIDGE

Left: This aerial view of the Chicago Skyway Bridge captures a moment in time along the 7.8-mile roadway built in 1958. The roadway swept travelers out to the southeast and then lifted them high above the Calumet River and Calumet Harbor on a suspension bridge unlike any other in town. The Skyway is a half-mile-long steel truss bridge, known locally as the "High Bridge." When the superhighway first opened it was known as the "Calumet Highway." Large amounts of revenue bonds were issued to pay the $101 million cost of construction. In 1960 the Dan Ryan Expressway opened and the Skyway was able to adapt and connect it to the Indiana Tollway.

Above: The construction of toll-free roadways made the Skyway lose money, which meant that it was unable to repay its revenue bonds. Traffic volume only increased once casinos started up over the Indiana border. In 2003 the City of Chicago began a $250 million rehabilitation project, widening the Chicago Skyway, as well as replacing the structural steel on the bridge. The city leased the rights to the Skyway Concession Company (SCC) and passed the maintenance bill in 2005. This marked the first time an American highway was leased by any governmental entity to a private company. Ironically, when Chicago first planned the Skyway, it discovered that it did not have the power to enact the construction of a toll road. It could only construct a "toll bridge." So, in fact, what it was able to construct was a toll bridge with a six-mile entrance ramp!

ORE DOCKS
BLAST FURNACES & STEEL MILLS
SOUTH CHICAGO ILL.
INTERNATIONAL HARVESTER CO.
CHICAGO ILL.

MERCHANT MILL NO.2

LABRATORY AND OFFICE

INTERNATIONAL HARVESTER ORE DOCKS

The South Works, with its accompanying ore docks and steel mills, shaped the footprint of a massive manufacturing company, International Harvester. Founded in Chicago in 1869 by William Deering, in its earliest days it was located along Fullerton Avenue. In 1902 Deering merged his company with the McCormick Harvesting Machine Company to become International Harvester. The new company bought a large piece of land in an industrial area, which was christened South Deering in 1903. There, Deering and his McCormick Harvester partners established what became known as Wisconsin Steel. This anchored the industrial development of the area, and many other industries set up there. Calumet Coal Company, Peoples Gas Light and Coke Company, Illinois Slag and Ballast Company, Chicago Steel and Iron, Gold Medal Flour (later General Mills), National Cylinder Gas Company, and the Chicago Iron and Coal Company all had remarkable success along the corridor of Torrence Avenue between 105th and 130th streets.

In an unprecedented measure in March 1980, Wisconsin Steel, by then owned by
Envirodyne Company, announced that it was closing its South Deering works. Without
any measure of compensation, 3,000 steel workers were let go. When the shift ended
one evening, padlocks were placed on all the gates in a shocking and irreversible
move by the owners. Blast furnaces were darkened. Envirodyne had no steelmaking
experience, and while they once planned a $50 million investment to upgrade, the
proposal never actually occurred. The loss of Wisconsin Steel was a serious economic
blow to Chicago and to the city's Southeast Side. Nearby Gary, Indiana, another steel
producer, presented a similar picture of stability and productivity. The economic
environment of the Deering community was badly damaged. The massive footprint of
the steel plant has remained empty. Recently, the City of Chicago announced plans
for a massive overhaul of the area with multitiered plans for commercial and
residential rebuilding.

NICHOLS BEACH / RAINBOW BEACH

Left: Some twenty-nine beaches dot the Chicago shoreline, rich with plentiful sand and white-capped freshwater—no salt here. When the beach located between Seventy-fifth and Seventy-eighth streets on the city's far South Side first opened, it was carefully maintained by a neighbor, George Nichols, whose house adjoined the beach. To all who used it, it was known as Nichols Beach, photographed here in 1906. By 1912 it had bathrooms and changing rooms, and remained open until 9:30 p.m. each night for the benefit of working Chicagoans. Its reputation as a pristine recreational area had already been earned. Expansion by the city in 1914 reshaped the shoreline here and created a broader beach front—most of it man-made, from old Nichols Beach and adjacent Rocky Ledge Beach to the south. A large public pier made this a favorite of South Siders, who flocked to the sandy shore in the blistering temperatures of a regular Chicago summer.

Above: In 1918 the Chicago City Council renamed the beach Rainbow Beach, honoring the U.S. Army's Forty-second Rainbow Division, which fought with distinction in World War I. The pier at Nichols Beach is long gone and so are the wool one-piece bathing suits. Chicago is boastful of its beaches and insists that it has the cleanest urban waterfront anywhere in the United States. Rainbow Beach is among the city's largest lakefront playgrounds. In the center of the frame is the Seventy-eighth Street pumping station, a facility that connects to the intake system of the city's water supply. Water is drawn not along the shoreline but at intake cribs far out in the lake, where water is purified before being sent to the pumping stations around the city. From these stations it goes directly to people's homes. Nearby Rocky Ledge Park provides spectacular views of both the Chicago skyline and the sweeping lakefront.

JACKSON PARK

Left: Jackson Park, named for America's seventh president, Andrew Jackson, is a 500-acre urban greenscape hugging the curvature of Lake Michigan along Chicago's southern coast. Frederick Law Olmsted, creator of New York's Central Park, joined architect Daniel Burnham in 1890 to lay out the shape and grandeur of this area for the 1893 World's Columbian Exhibition, or World's Fair. Six months after the fair closed, the area was returned to its parkland magnificence. Even as far back as 1899, the park boasted the nation's first public golf course west of the Allegheny Mountains. This aerial photo from 1936 is long after the 1924 "crime of the century" in which Nathan Leopold and Richard Loeb, both wealthy University of Chicago students, murdered fourteen-year-old Bobby Franks in a thrill killing. They threw the typewriter on which their crude ransom note to Frank's parents had been typed into the lagoon here in Jackson Park. Chicago's oldest and largest beach house for bathers stands at Sixty-third Street. Back in 1913 this beach was the site of the uproar that led to the arrest of Dr. Rosalie Ladova for removing the skirt of her bathing costume and swimming in her bloomers.

Above: Jackson Park today has more high-rise condos lining the sandy shoreline of Lake Michigan. It is just one of Chicago's 552 parks, though Jackson Park has little competition for size and beauty. The Jackson Park Yacht Club is among the most elegant in the city. South Shore Drive and Lake Shore Drive meander through the intricate system of Olmsted's park roads. Today, a few elements of the 1893 World's Fair remain—the Statue of the Republic by sculptor Daniel Chester French (one-third the size of the centerpiece of the fair) is still brightly gilded; and La Rabida, a lakeside promontory named for the site from which Columbus departed Spain. This was a focal point during the 1893 fair. Replicas of Columbus's three ships moored here during the fair. Today, a noted children's hospital, also named La Rabida, is housed here. Jackson Park is rich with bird trails, gardens, and tall grass. The Midway Plaisance is still the "bridge of green" that connects Jackson Park to Washington Park with its old English sheep's meadow and forest of great oak trees that have grown high following Olmsted's design.

W 63RD ST

MUNICIPAL AIRPORT /
MIDWAY AIRPORT

Left: The 320-acre slot of land for the Chicago Municipal Airport sat on the edge of the prairie when it opened very humbly in 1923, long before thousands of homes sprang up in the surrounding neighborhoods. Previously, there was only a small runway in Grant Park along the lakefront, before the age of commercial airlines. But after an airship crashed into the Illinois Trust and Savings Bank on LaSalle Street, killing thirteen people, air routes over downtown were abolished. The Municipal Airport began with just one runway, but by 1931 a new passenger terminal was built and air traffic increased, earning it the nickname of the "World's Busiest Airport," as more than 100,000 people passed through its portals each year. Chicago's central geographical location made it an ideal stopover, especially during an age of smaller aircraft and the necessity of frequent refueling on long flights. The main photograph was taken in 1936 and the inset dates to the early 1950s.

Above: The airport was renamed to honor the historic Battle of Midway, a turning point during World War II in the Pacific. Midway's growth made it highly congested, and there was little room for expansion. Mayor Richard J. Daley and Chicago aviation officials looked for suitable property outside the city limits capable of carrying the city into a new era of aviation. They selected a small airport northwest of the city called Orchard Field. Renamed as O'Hare International Airport to honor Lieutenant Commander Edward Henry "Butch" O'Hare, a Chicago aviation hero in World War II, it opened for regular passenger traffic in 1955. By 1961 O'Hare had surpassed Midway in the number of passengers served and Midway relinquished its title as the "World's Busiest Airport." With the critical addition of a transit line from downtown in 1993 and extraordinary investment in the infrastructure of the facility, Midway, with five runways, is returning in popularity and in the number of daily flights.

STOCKYARDS

Left: Chicago's Union Stock Yards opened on Christmas Day 1865, and over the next hundred years had a deep impact on the life and character of the city, especially in odor. It was the introduction of refrigerated railcars that ultimately put this livestock center on the map and changed the eating habits of the world. Situated between Forty-seventh Street on the south, Thirty-ninth Street on the north, Halsted Street (800 West) on the east, and Ashland Avenue (1600 West) on the west, it was a source of employment for immigrants who made their way to Chicago in the decades after the Great Fire of 1871. Cattle, pigs, and sheep were brought by rail to the stockyards where they were skinned, trimmed, and butchered. The meat was then placed aboard refrigerated railcars at nearby junctions and shipped worldwide. The main photograph was taken in 1936; the inset view is circa 1930.

Above: The packing houses are long gone and the aroma of animal matter no longer fills the Chicago air. Swift and Armour vacated their slaughterhouses in the 1950s and headed west. It made more economic sense to slaughter livestock where they were raised. Changes in American transportation, such as the growth of interstate trucking, helped dissipate the old enterprise. The culture that grew up around the stockyards is long gone, along with the common bonds shared among entire neighborhoods of Polish, Irish, and Lithuanian residents whose livelihood was made there. In 1971 the old footprint of the stockyards became known as the Stockyards Industrial Park. Few structures remain from the old days as new small manufacturing grows and flourishes there. All that remains is the triple limestone "Gateway of the Stockyards" at Halstead and Root streets, designed by Daniel Burnham and John Wellborn Root.

McKINLEY PARK

Left: McKinley Park, seen here in 1936, is a sixty-nine-acre city park honoring President William McKinley, assassinated at the Pan-American Exposition in Buffalo, New York, in 1901. This park was actually an experiment at providing park facilities in neighborhoods of high industrial character. McKinley Park sat on the edge of the Union Stock Yards, an area that was ripe for this kind of social intervention. The park provided ball fields, a swimming lagoon, playgrounds, changing rooms, and bathrooms—all aimed at influencing the development of local children. This project was so successful that it led to ten new Chicago-style parks spreading around the nation. Along Thirty-ninth Street are the buildings that once housed the Spiegel catalog company. Behind it at the top of the photo is a panorama of the Chicago Stockyards, behind the Chicago Junction Railroad Ashland Avenue Yards.

Above: Neither Chicago's Union Stock Yards nor Spiegel survived to the twenty-first century. The meatpacking industry had left Chicago by the 1960s for cities such as Omaha, Nebraska. The livestock industry vanished and the land has been redeveloped for other commercial uses. The railroad land that buffers the area between the stockyards and the Spiegel site has become one of the nation's largest intermodal freight yards, receiving millions of tons of movable goods by rail and truck and distributing them across the nation. But throughout the transition, McKinley Park has continued to thrive with tennis courts, a swimming pool, an ice-skating rink, and a soccer field. The Chicago Park District opened this recreation space located between Thirty-seventh Street and Pershing Road (Thirty-ninth Street), and between Western Avenue and Damen Avenue, as an experiment and discovered the future use of parks in the process.

FREDERICK ROBIE HOUSE

Left: The Robie House, at 5757 South Woodlawn Avenue, might just be Chicago architect Frank Lloyd Wright's finest Prairie-style residence. At over 9,000 square feet, it certainly remains one of his most expansive domestic designs. When Frederick C. Robie, an executive with the Schwinn Bicycle Company, engaged Wright, he stipulated that the house had to be built for $60,000—an enormous sum in 1906. Extravagant cantilevered roof eaves project like the deck of an aircraft carrier and give the structure its dramatic horizontal planes. So far-reaching was the long stretch of the house that special steel beams had to be fabricated to reach well over 100 feet in length. The exterior cladding is thin orange-red Roman brick, a telltale characteristic of Wright's designs. Wright lifted the window design high above the eyesight of anyone passing by. Light filled the interior through Wright's special geometric-shaped colored glass within the window treatments. As usual, every aspect of the interior—from furniture to carpets to appliances—was designed by Wright. This photograph dates to 1922.

Above: Financial difficulties and the failure of the Robies' marriage gave them little time in the house. Today, the Robie House is owned by the University of Chicago, within whose campus the building sits. It enjoys a unique pedigree in this unusual academic environment. After a series of private owners, the building had passed into the hands of a variety of academic owners and at one point was earmarked to be torn down and replaced with a dormitory. Local political leaders saw to it that the Robie House was made a Chicago landmark. It even survived for a while as a fraternity house. In the 1960s, the building was donated to the University of Chicago, which placed offices within it. In January 1997, the university turned over the house to the Frank Lloyd Wright Preservation Trust, which initiated plans for a historic restoration. The Robie House remains one of Wright's most evocative Prairie-style structures, infused with a nobility that was decades ahead of its time. Wright was not only a virtuoso in the design of good architecture, he was changing how Americans lived.

THE UNIVERSITY OF CHICAGO

Despite its roots as a Baptist university, the University of Chicago should be known as "Rockefeller University," but old John D. Rockefeller, the oil baron, wanted no self-aggrandizing in return for his financial investment. The University of Chicago is anchored into the Chicago neighborhood of Hyde Park/Kenwood, a community that has been shaped by the expansive growth of Chicago's most prestigious academic institution. Neo-Gothic was the operative design form in the decades immediately after its founding. But even as early as 1908, modern design entered the neighborhood when Frank Lloyd Wright designed the Robie House. While its modernity may appear complementary to the flying buttresses nearby, it was a jarring sight a century ago. Hyde Park's origins date back to the 1850s, but it was really the birth of the university that portended extraordinary things to come. The World's Fair put the surroundings on the map in 1893, but it was the university that would carry it to grandeur. The Midway Plaisance remains the green runway of the community and divides the university in half—north and south. The Quadrangles are architect Henry Ives Cobb's legacy of refinement to the campus, as well as the first buildings designed for university use. Mitchell Tower replicates Magdalen Tower at Oxford University and the University Commons (Hutchinson Hall) duplicates Christ Church Hall, Oxford. The Rockefeller Memorial Chapel is perhaps the most well-known Gothic structure on the campus. Designed by Bertram Goodhue, whose small stone image guards the east door, it has been a large part of campus life since it opened in 1928, a year before this photo was taken. Although the university's character is urban, this is a leafy pocket of Oxbridge-style beauty. The Oriental Institute, an oasis filled with rarefied artifacts, was founded in 1919.

Frederick Law Olmsted's lagoons are still intact within the park setting of the old fairgrounds. The Midway Plaisance is Chicago's most beautiful linear park, but today marks the dividing line between the north and south portions of the campus at the University of Chicago. George Ferris's wheel was rebuilt in Lincoln Park and became a big attraction after the fair, much to the annoyance of newspaper magnate William D. Boyce, who tried unsuccessfully to obtain a court order to have it moved. In 1904 it reopened in St. Louis at the centennial of the Louisiana Purchase Exhibition. It was dismantled in 1906 and a portion of the iron was used to build a bridge over the Kankakee River outside Chicago. After the fair closed in 1893, Ferris claimed that the exhibition management had robbed him and his investors of their rightful portion of the nearly $750,000 profit that his wheel brought in. He spent the next two years in litigation and died suddenly of typhoid fever in 1896 at the age of thirty-seven.

COMISKEY PARK / U.S. CELLULAR FIELD

Above: Comiskey Park was built as "the Baseball Palace of the World," as founder Charles Comiskey had called it—on land purchased in 1908 at Thirty-fifth Street and Shields Avenue. Comiskey made a promise to Sox fans that everyone would have a seat as good as any Chicago alderman. When it opened on July 1, 1910, nearly 30,000 people turned out and the *Chicago Tribune* called it "the greatest baseball plant in the world." It must have been the double-decker grandstand that caught everyone's attention. To many it looked like a great ocean liner. Comiskey built the stadium for an eye-popping $750,000, a monstrous price tag then. More than 16,000 fans could sit under the great sweeping roof. Because of the massive size of the playing field—363 feet down the foul lines and 420 feet out to center field—fans were spellbound by what they saw. It would be seventeen years before any player hit a home run out of the park. That player was Babe Ruth who slammed the ball more than 474 feet to clear the stadium wall.

Right: Nancy Faust, the White Sox organist, played the team's unofficial victory song at the last game of the season in 1990. Fans stayed around so everyone could sing "Auld Lang Syne." It was a heartbreaking moment for the 42,849 fans in attendance and for the thousands of Sox fans across the city. At one point, many of those present began to throw white socks onto the field. Today, the ground on which Charlie Comiskey's park sat is a garage and parking lot. U.S. Cellular Field opened for the 1991 season and the hallowed stadium was pulled down that same year. The inset image from 1991 shows the two stadiums side by side. A marble plaque on the sidewalk now shows the position of Comiskey Park's home plate, and the old foul lines are marked out on the lot.

EIGHTEENTH STREET BRIDGE

Left: The South Branch of the Chicago River—the longer of the river's two tributaries—is a maze of bridges because of the heavy railway presence, as well as city street traffic. The Eighteenth Street Railroad Bridges, in the lower right of the photo, are two rail bridges, each made of riveted metal, one being the longest bascule bridge in the world when built in 1919 for the Baltimore and Ohio Railroad. Continuing up the photo is the Eigteenth Street Vehicle Bridge, just beside the white-brick warehouse at the center of the frame. The 1906 Cermak Road Bridge (top) is the only Scherzer (rocking) rolling lift bridge in Chicago. Just beyond it is the Cermak Road Railroad Overpass Bridge (also known as the Chinatown Railroad Bridge), built for the New York Central railway and considered the finest overpass bridge in the city. Also in the frame are the old Canal Street Bridge, the only Vertical Lift Bridge near downtown, and the 1915 Canal Street Railroad Bridge by Waddell and Harrington. The Illinois and Michigan Canal, which joined the river at Thirty-fifth Street and Archer Avenue, is more than a mile in the distance in the Bridgeport neighborhood.

Above: The Illinois and Michigan Canal—where the Irish diggers stopped and took their payment in land—has long since ceased to function. However, the Bridgeport neighborhood produced five Chicago mayors in the twentieth century. Chicago's economic viability switched to railroads in the 1850s. But the South Branch did maintain an important waterway for the small shipment of goods like ore and quarried rock. The project to straighten the Chicago River in the 1920s reconfigured many of the South Branch's bridge overpasses. The Taylor Street Bridge was removed altogether. The land to the left of the picture is all landfill, formerly the original path of the river before 1929. The Eighteenth Street Railroad Bridge was 260 feet long when first built. After the river was moved a quarter of a mile to the west, the bridge was shortened by forty feet. The lanes of the Stevenson Expressway, which follow the pathway of the canal, added concrete over some of the waterway many years ago.

WORLD'S FAIR OF 1933

Left: The buildings of Chicago's 1893 World's Fair were fashioned in the neoclassical style; in 1933 they were all sleek, metallic Art Deco. This photo, looking north toward the soaring Chicago skyline, shows the Century of Progress on October 26, 1933—the day that Germany's new chancellor, Adolf Hitler, sent the helium passenger dirigible, the *Graf Zeppelin*, replete with swastikas, to the fair. At the top of the frame is the fair's most exciting attraction—the Sky Ride. Passengers rode in rocketlike gondolas, suspended on cables stretched between two 628-foot towers. Passengers rode 219 feet above the ground. The photo is taken from Thirty-fifth Street at the far southern end of the fairgrounds, where the Ukrainian Pavilion was located; nearby is the tented area holding the Poultry Show and the Domestic Animal Show. At the center right is the Thirty-first Street Boat Landing facilitated water transportation to the fair.

Above: The southern lakefront still holds the configuration of the 1933 World's Fair, greener now more than ever. The expansion of Chicago's downtown commercial and residential buildings is profound. But at the center of the upper sight lines is McCormick Place, resembling an aircraft carrier; to its left is McCormick Place 2, along with two further buildings—McCormick Places 3 and 4—with 2.6 million square feet of exhibition space, 1.2 million of which is all on one level. It is the nation's largest exposition center for conventions. Close to 3 million visitors come to the conventions and exhibits at McCormick Place each year.

WORLD'S FAIR OF 1933

Left: The 1933 Century of Progress stretched across the Chicago lakefront southward for three and a half miles and was a World's Fair to remember. For Chicagoans, it bucked the trend of the Great Depression and gave a lift to the low spirits of the times. Among the more popular sites at the fair was the Hall of Science (bottom center of photo), the nearby Time Magazine Pavilion and Fortune Magazine Pavilion, and the *City of New York* (in the waters of Lake Michigan at the upper right), the vessel on which Admiral Richard E. Byrd sailed to the Antarctic, just beside the Havoline Thermometer. Also popular were the pavilions located on Northerly Island, which stretches across the upper left of the image. Here was the Electricity Exhibit; the Enchanted Island for Children with a children's restaurant, theater, and castle; and the Horticultural Exhibit. Visitors also saw Cadillac's first V-16 limousine, a 1936 Lincoln-Zephyr with a front engine, a Silver Arrow Pierce-Arrow, and the Packard, which won best of show. Another popular attraction was the 1933 Homes of Tomorrow exhibit.

Above: Northerly Island, which once anchored many of the fair's popular pavilions, and the land at Twenty-second Street, the spot where McCormick Place sits today, are the only relics of the old fair's imprint. Burnham Harbor, an important part of the lakefront's recreational character, today sits at the center of what was the fair's past footprint. Some of the structures that were a part of the Homes of Tomorrow exhibit were removed in sections and shipped across the lake to the Indiana Dunes when the fair closed, and were refitted as beach houses. Many are still there today. Though the Shedd Aquarium and the Adler Planetarium were not officially constructed as exhibits for the fair, having been open to the public before the fair began, their proximity to the fair made them very popular sites among fairgoers.

WORLD'S FAIR OF 1933

Left: Forty-eight million people visited the fair in 1933 and 1934, celebrating the 100th anniversary of Chicago's incorporation as a city in 1833. The footprint of the fair was placed on Northerly Island, one of Daniel Burnham's anchor islands along the lakefront. It also utilized the land surrounding what is today known as Burnham Harbor, the vicinity of Twelfth Street and Lake Shore Drive, near Soldier Field, stretching as far south as Thirty-ninth Street. The fair's theme—"Science Finds, Industry Applies, Man Conforms"—set the tone of the international gathering on 427 acres along shimmering Lake Michigan. In this photo, the United States Pavilion features three soaring columns representing the three branches of American government—the executive, the legislative, and the judicial. Across the waterway is the John G. Shedd Aquarium. Among the notable events of the fair was the arrival of the fascist Italian aviator general, Italo Balbo, who arrived with a squadron of Mussolini's air force navigating across the Atlantic.

Above: Some of the biggest hits at the fair included Sally Rand, the famous fan dancer, Judy Garland, and the Andrews Sisters. After World War II, Northerly Island was designated as the site of a new airport that came to be known as Meigs Field, named for the publisher Merrill C. Meigs, of the *Herald-Examiner* newspaper. Meigs Field provided aircraft with the opportunity to land close to downtown Chicago. General Italo Balbo's column (out of frame, to the left) continues to stand in Burnham Harbor on a base of travertine marble, more than seventy-five years after its arrival. The column commemorates Balbo's transatlantic flight, from Rome to Chicago, in 1933. His name is still in use along nearby Balbo Drive. Charter One Pavilion still serves as a venue for concerts during the summer months. Following the close of the fair, Chicago added another red star on the municipal flag in honor of the Century of Progress.

McCORMICK PLACE

This view from Northerly Island to McCormick Place shows the footprint of the Museum Campus as the reconfigured landscape holding McCormick Place, Soldier Field, the Chicago Police Memorial, the Field Museum of Natural History, the Adler Planetarium, and the Shedd Aquarium. As far back as the late 1920s, the *Chicago Tribune*'s owner, Robert R. McCormick, championed the cause of a dedicated lakeside convention center for Chicago. The Great Depression, World War II, and the postwar recovery program intervened, but in 1958 ground was broken for a $35 million facility on land visible in the 1926 archive photo of Soldier Field (see page 62). The exposition hall opened in November 1960, five years after McCormick's death. It was destroyed by fire in 1967 and a subsequent investigation gained new insights into how a seemingly fireproof building of steel and concrete could be vulnerable to a fire. The associated Arie Crown Theatre sustained only minor damage and was able to be incorporated into the replacement building, which opened in 1971. The northbound lanes of Lake Shore Drive, which formerly ran east of many of these structures, was diverted in 1998 to run west of them, creating a fifty-seven-acre park. The removal of the roadway shaped a remarkable urban green space through which visitors and Chicago residents can walk contiguously free of traffic along the lakefront through Grant Park and Millennium Park—from Twenty-second Street to Randolph Street. An expanded Shedd Aquarium is now among the lakefront's most stunning attractions, boasting the world's largest indoor aquarium with 25,000 fish in five million gallons of seawater. It also houses a Komodo dragon named Faust. The Oceanarium holds beluga whales.

SOLDIER FIELD

Soldier Field takes up a lot of space in Chicago's history. It first opened on October 9, 1924, along the waters of Lake Michigan and was originally known as Municipal Grant Park Stadium. William Holabird and Martin Roche, the architects who designed many Chicago buildings of grandeur and stature, designed this remarkable neoclassical-inspired Greco-Roman columned stadium. Recognizing the great debt owed to the soldiers who had sacrificed so much on the battlefieds of World War I just six years earlier, the official name of the stadium was changed to Soldier Field on Armistice Day, November 11, 1926. The first ball game played there was football, appropriately an Army-Navy game, on November 27, 1926, seen here photographed from the roof of the Natural History Museum looking south. The inset photo was taken at the same game looking north. The contours and lines of the structure had a profoundly elegant character, as well as enormous physical size. Upon completion, the stadium had 74,280 seats, and with the addition of temporary bleachers, the stadium could hold 110,000 for their inaugural game.

Soldier Field, home to the Chicago Bears football team since 1971, underwent massive renovation of the stadium in 2003 that was both extensive and controversial. While retaining the signature colonnade that wraps around the complex, a whole new stadium was constructed within the old stadium's design. It has been referred to as "a spaceship landing on the old stadium," yet many applaud both the design and the continued outdoor exposure of what remains professional football's smallest stadium. Soldier Field lost its historic landmark status in 2006 as a result of the renovation, which reduced the seating to 61,500.

SOLDIER FIELD

An aerial view of the stadium reveals the modern infrastructure of the multitiered seating nestled between the historic colonnades. Situated along Lake Shore Drive, Soldier Field can boast about its nearby neighbors of equal neoclassical elegance—the Field Museum designed by Daniel Burnham; the Shedd Aquarium by Graham, Anderson, Probst and White; and the Adler Planetarium by Ernest Grunsfeld. Owned by the Chicago Park District, Soldier Field cost $10 million to build. In 1927 former boxing champion Jack Dempsey defeated world heavyweight champion Gene Tunney in a ten-round unanimous decision. On June 18, 1933, a student from East Technical High School in Cleveland, Ohio, set an unparalleled mark when he tied the world record for the 100-yard dash. The time of 9.4 seconds was sensational at a National Interscholastic Track and Field meet. The athlete was Jesse Owens, and three years later he would go on to collect four gold medals at the 1936 Berlin Olympic Games: the 100-meter dash, 200-meter dash, long jump, and 4 x 100–meter relay. Owens later lived in Chicago and is buried in Oak Woods Cemetery here. Chicago continues to cherish its lakefront presence and the steady ability to host international music events like the Grateful Dead in 1995 (Jerry Garcia's last show) and U2's 2009 world tour. Soldier Field has the distinction of hosting the very first Special Olympic Games on July 20, 1968.

FIELD MUSEUM OF NATURAL HISTORY

Above: The Field Museum of Natural History is shown here on October 26, 1933, as the *Graf Zeppelin* circles in the skies above. The original natural history museum opened in the fall of 1893 as the Columbian Museum, using the World's Fair building known as the Palace of Fine Arts (see page 39). It moved to its new home here at Fourteenth Street and Lake Shore Drive in 1921. Built with funds from the estate of Chicago department store king Marshall Field, the facility is dedicated to natural science, archaeology, and history. The building was designed by Daniel Burnham and Company in a classical-revivalist style. Among the most prominent specimens in the museum collection are the lions of Tsavo, who once terrorized the construction of the Uganda-Mombasa Railway in 1898—an event that provided the premise for the award-winning film *The Ghost and the Darkness*. Nearby, on the adjacent right, is the John G. Shedd Aquarium, opened in 1930. Both these attractions had high visibility during the World's Fair of 1933.

Right: The Field Museum is still a popular Chicago attraction. Sue, the most complete Tyrannosaurus in the world, keeps company with the woolly mammoths in the Great Hall and greets all who enter the Field Museum. On the floor below, at the central axis of the ground level, is the massive collection of artifacts from Ancient Egypt, including a rich harvest of mummies from the era of Field Museum archeological digs. The galleries are also rich in the antiquity of the Native peoples of the Pacific Northwest, a specialty of Field Museum study; Tibetan cultural antiquity; as well a vast collection of Native American artifacts. The museum also holds 7,000 volumes on Asian anthropology and archaeology. A photo archive holds more than 250,000 images in the natural sciences and, of course, a vast array of images from the World's Columbian Exposition, to which this museum is a living reminder.

GRANT PARK LAKEFRONT

Top: Railroad tracks east of Michigan Avenue dominate the foreground of this panorama of the Grant Park lakefront. Many buildings still familiar to Chicagoans filled the streetscape on the west side of Michigan Avenue. Extreme left is the Blackstone Hotel (1908); farther down on the left is the Auditorium Building complex (1887), an opera house, hotel, and office block. Architects Dankmar Adler and Louis Sullivan had their office in the building's tower. It was America's tallest building at the time of the 1893 World's Fair. Next door is the Studebaker Building (1895). One full block north is the Santa Fe Railway Building (1903) and Orchestra Hall (1889). Across the street from the low-rising Art Institute of Chicago (1893) is the People's Gas Building (1911) at Adams Street; the University Club (1908) at Monroe Street, next door to the Gage Building (1898); the Montgomery Ward Building Tower (1897) at Madison; and the Public Library (1897). These are finely crafted buildings fashioned by some of America's best architects—all of whom made their reputations and their homes in Chicago. This stunning streetscape and parkland demonstrates the important role that buildings of merit were to play in Chicago's self-understanding as a metropolis.

Bottom: The ebullient Grant Park footprint is even more spectacular than the image from a hundred years ago. Remarkably, all of the pre-1911 structures previously noted are still in use. Around them, the streets are thick with new buildings, none more bold than the 1973 Willis Tower (formerly the Sears Tower) at 233 South Wacker Drive. Known as the tallest building in the United States, at 108 floors and 1,451 feet high (with antenna, 1,730 feet), it was designed by the architectural firm Skidmore, Owings, and Merrill.

A BIRDS-EYE VIEW OF CHICAGO FROM ELEVATION 700 ft. ABOVE LAKE MICHIGAN.

GRANT PARK AND SKYLINE

The contours of Grant Park's botanical elegance are without equal in Chicago. The park's centerpiece is the 1927 Buckingham Fountain (center and inset), a gift from philanthropist Kate Buckingham in memory of her brother, Clarence. The fountain was fashioned of Georgia pink marble and deeply influenced by the Latona Basin at Versailles. Edward H. Bennett designed the structure and placed four large sea horses within it to symbolize Wisconsin, Illinois, Indiana, and Michigan—the four states that touch Lake Michigan. Bennett's hand guided much of Grant Park's elegant design and other lakefront amenities. Nearby are the bronze 1928 Indian warriors—the *Bowman* and the *Spearman*—that sit atop large columns at the Congress Parkway entrance designed by famed sculptor Ivan Mestrovic. The park runs from Roosevelt Road on the south to Randolph on the north, and Michigan Avenue to the lakeshore. The Art Institute of Chicago remains the only building aboveground east of Michigan Avenue. It looms on the landscape more than ever with the 2009 addition of its Modern Wing designed by the renowned international architect Renzo Piano. The Agora statues, 106 rusted cast-iron sculptures, each nine feet tall, are an artistic shock for many Grant Park visitors. They are modern and edgy and were fashioned by Magdalena Abakanowicz and placed in the park in 2006. The panorama of this photo displays Chicago's most stunning architectural buildings from a wide period of design including the 1,450-foot tall Willis Tower built in 1973 with 110 stories of black Cor-Ten steel. The Museum Campus, the fifty-seven acres surrounding the Adler Planetarium, the Shedd Aquarium, and the Field Museum of Natural History sit at the park's southern end. Millennium Park sits at the north. In addition, there are sixteen softball fields and twelve tennis courts. Grant Park is the home to many Chicago festivals, including Taste of Chicago, Chicago Blues Festival, Celtic Fest, the Chicago Jazz Festival, and Lollapalooza.

ART INSTITUTE OF CHICAGO

The Art Institute of Chicago has a long and historic relationship with the Chicago metropolis. It is America's second-largest art museum, after the Metropolitan Museum of Art in New York. Established just eight years after the Great Fire of 1871, its presence ever since demonstrates a sense of refined aesthetics on the flatland of the prairie. That was especially true in the rougher eras of nineteenth-century settlement. The Art Institute moved to its present permanent home at 11 S. Michigan Avenue in 1893, just after the close of the World's Fair. The building was the fair's only off-site pavilion. The World Parliament of Religions was housed here for six months. After they vacated the premises, some of the art from Palace of Fine Arts was moved to the Art Institute's new home. Bertha Palmer, Chicago's leading social maven, helped to fill the walls with some of her collection of French Impressionists and post-Impressionist art. Following her death in 1916, her entire collection was placed here, making Chicago the largest center for such refined and modern works outside of Paris. Standing guard at its Michigan Avenue entrance—and very much a part of the Chicago landscape—are two bronze lions designed by Edwards Kemeys. This photograph is from 1923.

Today the Art Institute of Chicago is more dynamic and more robust than ever. The main Michigan Avenue entrance displays the refinements of design by the architectural firm of Shepley, Rutan, and Coolidge. Over the ensuing years there has been a significant expansion to the east, but nothing compares to the recent completion of architect Renzo Piano's Modern Wing—a 264,000-square-foot addition opened in spring 2009. Housed here is the museum's extraordinary twentieth-century European art collection. Also added were shops and a restaurant, Terzo Piano, which overlooks Millennium Park. A bridgeway designed by architectural firm Gustafson Guthrie Nichol connects the rooftop sculpture garden of the Modern Wing to nearby Millennium Park. Grant Wood's *American Gothic*, Pablo Picasso's *The Old Guitarist*, Gustave Caillebotte's *Paris Street, Rainy Day*, and Georges Seurat's *A Sunday Afternoon on the Island of La Grande Jatte* are some of the most popular paintings in the collection. South Michigan Avenue has expanded into a residential neighborhood with many returning suburbanites relocating to the city in the converted commercial high-rises. New restaurants fill the streets and cater to an artsy crowd, not only from the Art Institute, but also from the nearby Symphony Center.

EAST OF MICHIGAN AVENUE

Left: Chicago's legacy as America's rail hub created a network of rail lines that carried freight and passengers in every direction. In the city's early days, most of those tracks were placed along the lakefront. This photo of a pre-skyscraper landscape showcases the massive confluence of tracks east of Michigan Avenue. The photo also details the vast areas of empty space north of the river. The construction of the Wrigley Building and the Tribune Tower in the 1920s heralded the advent of urban design for the streets north of the river. Buildings of note were soon a part of the landscape. Under the leadership of Mayor Edward Kelly in the 1930s, Chicago's urban expansion was powerful, not only in scope, but in its aesthetical balance. The old industrial face of Chicago and its gritty railroads soon shared the landscape with modern office complexes and tailored streetscapes.

Above: It is difficult to find rail yards and railway storage facilities downtown today because of the sale of the air rights above them. This also allowed Chicago to expand with enormous success during the post–World War II years. Nothing demonstrates this more than the area surrounding the train tracks east of Michigan Avenue. The addition of a double-decker link-bridge over the eastern portion of the Chicago River in 1937 connected Lake Shore Drive on each side of the river and advanced the fast-paced urban expansion. A flourish of construction began there with the Prudential Building along Randolph Street in 1955. Later, the expansion of mixed-use development on the south side of the river at Wacker Drive increased with the Hyatt Regency Hotel, the Swiss Hotel, and One, Two, and Three Illinois Center. The bright red, forty-four-story, CNA Center (1972), has become a city landmark. Today the Illinois Central Railroad has expanded its rail station beneath Michigan Avenue and Randolph Street for commuter passengers to the southern suburbs and Indiana. Nearby Millennium Park further erased the rail beds that had long ago ceased operations.

MILLENNIUM PARK

Above: In the 1920s, the rage for auto transport was high and the empty space east of Michigan Avenue was the perfect open area on which to park the growing numbers of private automobiles. Grant Park looks more like a garage than a park in this photo before underground parking was built. Low-rise buildings from the late nineteenth century—like the Gage Building on the left and the public library toward the center—now share the streetscape with some of the most modern designs in the nation, like the thirty-eight-story, copper-roofed, Pittsfield Building (far left) opened in 1927. In the center of the frame, the tower of the 1926 Jewelers Building on Wacker Drive (with a massive domed-pavilion tower), and the tall, thin spire of the 1926 Mather Tower, also on Wacker Drive, soar above the city.

Right: This is the very heart of Millennium Park. Taken from beneath the tubular sound system of the Pritzker Music Pavilion designed by architect Frank Gehry, this photo offers a sweeping view of some classic skyscrapers: the forty-one-story Prudential Building (1955), the first commercial high-rise built since the Great Depression; the 995-foot tall Two Prudential Plaza (1990); and the Aon Center (1973), which at 1,136 feet is the third tallest building in Chicago. Millennium Park is a triumph of corporate giving that saw corporations like Boeing, AT&T, Wrigley Gum, Chase Bank, Crown Foundation, Exelon, and the *Chicago Tribune* extend remarkable generosity to underwrite the park's construction. Today, thousands of automobiles park here each day—all underground in the cavernous Grant Park Garage. Inset, left: Anish Kapoor's *Cloud Gate* (1999). Inset, right: The temporary Burnham Pavilion (2009) by Zaha Hadid Architects.

LAKE PARK AIR FIELD, GRANT PARK

Lake Park Air Field—a short-lived runway along the lakefront in Grant Park—was a place of urban excitement and wonder. Walter Brookins made the first flight from Lake Park in 1910, setting an important record. The Chicago Air Show Competition of August 12, 1911, is shown here, with the Wright Brothers' pusher aircraft a part of the day's events. Just to the north of the airstrip is the Chicago Public Library on Michigan Avenue between Washington and Randolph Streets, designed by the firm of Shepley, Rutan, and Coolidge in 1897, the largest mosaic building in the world next to the Hagia Sophia in Istanbul. The prominent tower, topped with a weathervane and soaring high on the west side of Michigan Avenue, is the headquarters of Montgomery Ward and Company, designed by Richard C. Schmidt in 1897. To the far left is the University Club, designed by Holabird and Roche in 1908. By the time of this photo, Michigan Avenue was already a brilliant urban streetscape of important architectural significance.

The use of the Lake Park Airstrip was short-lived. On July 21, 1919, the Goodyear Tire and Rubber Company's *Wingfoot Express* crashed into the Illinois Trust and Savings Bank in the center of the financial district of LaSalle Street shortly before the end of the business day. Fire rained from the sky and burned thirteen people alive in the atrium of the bank lobby. Public outrage at the airship disaster ended flights from the park and flights over the Loop, though plans were soon made to fashion a lakefront airport off the shoreline. Today, the empty land that was the airstrip is Millennium Park, one of the most beautiful in the nation boasting a variety of dramatic public sculptures, visited by tens of thousands of people each day. The library has become the Chicago Cultural Center, saved from destruction in 1991 by Mrs. Richard J. Daley, widow of the former mayor, when a new flagship library opened on State Street. The Montgomery Ward headquarters has been reconfigured as residential condominiums and the Gustafson Guthrie Nichol bridgeway can now be seen at this site linking the Modern Wing addition of the Art Institute over Monroe Street to Millennium Park. Few Chicagoans, if any, know of the former airstrip that once operated here.

MARINA CITY

The twin corn-cob towers of Marina City (left), designed by architect Bertrand Goldberg in the early 1960s, rise up on old railroad land long abandoned and unused along the river at State Street. No Chicagoan had ever seen anything so modern or more chic along the river when the 900-unit apartment complex that forms a city within a city of poured concrete arose. Self-sustaining and filled with every convenience—from dry cleaners to a bowling alley—it was the brainchild of Chicago's tough political boss Mayor Richard J. Daley, who saw Marina City as the chance to reshape the commercial downtown with residential high-rise living. Commissioned by the International Union of Janitors, whom Daley convinced of its urban importance, it held a full urban marina along the water. These scallop-shelled pie-wedges changed the way Chicagoans lived and the way that condos are built today. The ninety-six-story Trump International Hotel and Tower (center left) handsomely dominates the area of North Michigan Avenue and the Chicago River. Its sleek, shimmering contoured glass ushers in a new age of Chicago architecture as it takes its place as third-tallest high-rise on the urban grid. Opened in 2008, it carries on a tradition of elegant riverfront architectural design. The Wrigley Building and Tribune Tower began the great shift to commerce and recreation north of the river in the 1920s. With the addition of the doubled-decked Michigan Avenue Bridge in 1922, commerce across the river had a more equal footing.

WACKER DRIVE ESPLANADE

The Wacker Drive Esplanade is an expression of "the City Beautiful Movement." The movement was all about the increase in grandeur and elegance in design, and Chicago was a recipient of its goals. The World's Fair of 1893 is a prime example of the design concept of the movement, which showed at the fair the grandeur of neoclassical architectural design. The impact of the fair's design was significant around the city, nowhere more so than in the reshaping of the riverfront from Michigan Avenue west. The Wrigley Building (mirroring the lines of a Spanish cathedral) and the Tribune Tower (mirroring the style of a French cathedral), prominently featured in this photo,

were both revivalist styles when completed in the early 1920s. They were soon followed by others: the classicist style of the London Guarantee Trust Building on the south side of the river (right of center); behind it, the tall and narrow lantern spire of the Mather Tower; and the Jewelers Building (far right of the frame). These early additions to the Chicago skyline cemented the city's dedication to the refinements of revivalist styles on both sides of the Chicago River. The refinement of the riverscape was further strengthened by the appearance of Marshall Field's massive Merchandise Mart. These structures lifted the sightlines of the urban landscape.

The wide spaces that once could be seen between the riverscape's urban profile have disappeared. The additions of large numbers of new modernist designs have enriched the streetscape. Skidmore, Owings, and Merrill's Equitable Building (1965), at 401 North Michigan Avenue, sits left of center in this photo and is where John Kinzie, one of Chicago's first settlers, established his farm. In 1847 this was also the site on which Cyrus McCormick built his first reaper plant, which revolutionized the farming industry. The Seventeenth Church of Christ, Scientist (the low-rise triangular building, right of center), at 55 East Wacker Drive, was designed by Harry Weese and readjusts the sight-lines of the riverside. The Hotel 71 (left of the church), once known as the Executive House, brought an additional sense of modernism. And on the north side of the river, the IBM Building (far left of the frame) deepens the Miesian minimalism of the Chicago School of design, alongside the massive Trump International Hotel and Tower (second from left) that soars high and shimmers.

The excursion steamer *North American* is towed by a tug at the mouth of the Chicago River, ferrying passengers for a day's outing along the lakefront or across to Michigan City, Indiana, a favorite destination. The exciting "New York–style" 1920s skyline is prominently featured—from the sky-high steeple of Holabird and Roche's 1922 Chicago Temple Building (on the far left of the frame), to the stunning 1929 Carbon and Carbide Building (at the center top), alongside the 1924 Greek templelike Jewelers Building in which elevators carried automobiles up to tenants' offices, with the 1926 Mather Tower rising above everything to the right, and the 333 North Michigan Building from 1928. To the right, in the distance, on the north side of the river, is the 1931 Merchandise Mart by Graham, Anderson, Probst, and White. The Michigan Avenue Bridge, opened in 1920, spans the eastern end of the river. Its pylon towers were added in 1928.

CHICAGO RIVER MOUTH

Seen here in the raised position, the Columbus Drive Bridge—a single deck, box girder bridge—opened on October 31, 1982, and largely changed the way Chicago moves. This is the city's most eastern bridge and its construction facilitated the heavy development that has taken place east of Michigan Avenue during the past twenty years. From trunion to trunion, the bridge is 269 feet long (the same size as the Wabash Avenue Bridge) and is 111 feet at its widest point, standing twenty-one feet above the water. A new cityscape has risen at the river's mouth. The shimmering thirty-story Swiss Hotel (on the left), a triangular structure by Harry Weese and Associates, sits on land that was once a rail yard. Sixteen million square feet of office space and 7,500 hotel rooms sit

east of Michigan Avenue on the south side of the river, amid Ludwig Mies van der Rohe's One Illinois Plaza, the Hyatt Regency Hotel, and the lake. On the north side of the river, the forty-story City Front began the new residential shift in 1991 and continues with the fifty-four-story Parkview West completed in 2008. River traffic is more restrictive now than in past decades, but the bridges do open, particularly in the fall when boats make their way to boatyards along the South Branch. Lifts occur Wednesday and Saturdays starting at the lakefront, continuing down the Main and South river branches at 9:30 a.m. and 11:00 a.m. On Saturdays the bridges lift at 9:00 a.m. and 11:00 a.m., with each bridge lift lasting between eight and ten minutes.

THE *EASTLAND* DISASTER

Above: At 6:30 a.m. on July 24, 1915, employees of Western Electric Company began boarding the passenger steamer *Eastland* (inset) at the pier along the Chicago River between LaSalle and Clark streets to attend the company's fifth annual picnic. The excursion would take them across Lake Michigan to Michigan City, Indiana, for the day's festivities. In less than an hour, more than 2,700 passengers had climbed aboard, reaching the ship's capacity. The *Eastland* tilted to the port side, so the crew added ballast to stabilize it. When contestants in a canoe race along the river passed by, around 7:28 a.m., a large number of passengers on the upper deck rushed to the port side for a glance. At that moment, the ship completely tilted onto its port side, hurling everything and everybody onto its side into the river. Despite the best efforts of those nearby, more than 841 people perished in the twenty-feet-deep waters. Witnesses were in shock at the swiftness of the tragedy that befell the passengers—many were trapped in the water on the decks below, crushed by the weight of furniture and falling debris. A large majority of those aboard were Czech immigrants employed near their West Side homes.

Right: The *Eastland* was raised from the water, later sold to the Illinois Naval Reserve, and converted into a gun boat named the *Wilmette*. During World War II, in addition to serving as a training vessel, the *Wilmette* transported President Franklin Roosevelt for a wartime strategy planning session on the Great Lakes. In 1947 she was scrapped. The site of the *Eastland* disaster, along the north side of the Wacker Drive esplanade between LaSalle and Clark streets, holds a memorial placed there in 1995 for the eightieth anniversary of the tragedy. Libby Hruby, the last survivor of the *Eastland*, a ten-year-old girl at the time of the disaster, was present for the memorial. Today, the surrounding areas have been reshaped into some of the city's most beautiful walkways. The river, here, is thick with new skyscrapers and restored commercial structures from the past. And the waterway is busy with tour boats, water taxis, and sailboats making their way into Lake Michigan. The *Eastland* disaster remains the worst in U.S. maritime history for loss of life.

MICHIGAN AVENUE BRIDGE

Built in 1920, the Michigan Avenue Bridge was the first bridge to span the Chicago River at Michigan Avenue. It was designed by Edward H. Bennett, the Chicago architect who partnered with Daniel Burnham on the 1909 *Plan of Chicago*. This is Chicago's most important bascule bridge—a movable counterweighted bridge, one of thirty-six like it in the city that allow for boat traffic on the Chicago River. This bridge is actually two parallel bridges capable of independent action. Traffic flows on two separate levels. The bridge is 399 feet long, its main span is 220 feet long and 92 feet wide. Two 180-horsepower motors open and close the two 3,750-ton bridge leaves. This is the gateway to the "Magnificent Mile," as Michigan Avenue is known.

Michigan Avenue is thick with extraordinary botanicals, large leaf plants and wild floral plantings as far as the eye can see. A rich green thoroughfare unfolds along the sidewalks filled with flower boxes and huge urns spilling over in color and fragrance. The Michigan Avenue Bridge remains the gate to Chicago's ever-expanding cityscape and is surrounded by its most distinguished architecture—the London Guarantee Trust, the Wrigley Building, the Tribune Tower, the 333 N. Michigan Avenue Building, and the Equitable Building. Today the neighborhood stands in the shadow of Chicago's third tallest building, the Trump Tower complex. The architectural beauty of the Michigan Avenue Bridge is timeless and fits the evolving style of Chicago's skyline. Just east of the bridge further expansion has produced, on each side of the river, fresh development, like the NBC Tower, the University of Chicago Business School; as well as the "Water Arc," a water sculpture that commemorates the reversal of the Chicago River in 1900. Every hour on the hour an arc of water shoots across the expanse of the river's width for ten minutes. Nearby, also, are the Swiss Hotel and the Hyatt, each representing other eras of Chicago design, all balanced with the contours and the design of the Michigan Avenue Bridge's timeless splendor.

THE WRIGLEY BUILDING

The Wrigley Building stands as the doorway to Chicago's near-North Side, beside the Michigan Avenue Bridge that carries traffic across what might be the city's most elegant river crossing, based on the fashionable Alexander III Bridge across the Seine in Paris. The Wrigley Building looms large near the site of Old Fort Dearborn built in 1803. Designed by the firm of Graham, Anderson, Probst, and White, the Wrigley Building is a glistening white, terra-cotta wedding cake of a design patterned after the Giralda Tower of the Cathedral of Seville, with some added French renaissance design details. Opened in 1921, the Wrigley Building is actually two buildings of differing heights, with the south building rising to thirty stories and the north to twenty-one. The building's second section was completed in 1924. Linked at two floors by bridges, it has the distinction of being the first air-conditioned building in Chicago. The great clock features four dials, one in each direction allowing people from all directions to see the time. The building served as headquarters of the Wrigley Chewing Gum Company, having been commissioned by its founder William Wrigley Jr. The Wrigley Building has been traditionally illuminated at night by special tiers of lights that accentuate its white cladding. It was set on land that was once the homestead of Jean Baptiste Pointe du Sable, an early French Haitian settler who was known as "the Father of Chicago," having been declared the city's founder.

The Wrigley Building has been an anchor of the riverfront and Michigan Avenue since its start as a growing commercial area. In fact, its construction on the north side of the Chicago River became a powerful catalyst for growth along North Michigan Avenue. In addition to the Wrigley Chewing Gum Company, the building has been the traditional home to many advertising firms in the great era of that profession's boom. It has also been the home of some diplomatic missions, like the Irish and British Consulates. The Wrigley Building remains a Chicago favorite, and many regular Chicagoans place it at the top of their list of the city's best architectural designs. It has been the jewel of the "Magnificent Mile," which was previously known as "Boul Mich" because Michigan Avenue had once been named Michigan Boulevard. Together, the Wrigley Building along with the Tribune Tower, on the east side of Michigan Avenue, created a handsome architectural gateway that raised the bar on design of fashionable, timeless architecture.

CITY HALL / COURTHOUSE SQUARE

Left: The Cook County Courthouse and City Hall building was designed in 1853 by John M. Van Osdel. It is pictured inset with mourners filing into the building in May 1865 to pay their respects to slain President Abraham Lincoln before his burial in the Illinois State capital of Springfield, Illinois—Lincoln's hometown. More than 125,000 people filed by his casket. This was Chicago's fourth city hall and sat in what was called Courthouse Square, the property between LaSalle and Clark streets and Washington and Randolph streets. For the time period, with two domes and a cupola, this was elaborate, grandiose architecture, though only three stories high before the addition of another floor in 1858. The building was constructed out of buff granite from the quarries of nearby Lockport, Illinois. The first floor contained most of the city's offices. The second was the home of the Chicago City Council Chambers. The third was home to the Cook County Surveyor, the City Surveyor, and the City Superintendent. Trade and manufacturing during this period made many Chicagoans wealthy and created a boom culture within the city.

Above: The building did not survive the Great Chicago Fire of 1871. However, out of the ashes of Courthouse Square, two more city halls/county buildings have risen on the footprint of Van Osdel's structure. A sixth complex was built from 1885 until 1909; and the present seventh structure was completed in 1911. Designed in the architectural flourish of a neoclassical Greek temple by the architectural firm of Holabird and Roche, muscular Corinthian columns give a soaring vertical lift to the lines of the massing. Seen here, the eastern half of the structure on the Clark Street side, is the home of offices of the Cook County government. The LaSalle Street side on the west houses the central government of the City of Chicago, including its third-floor city council chambers and fifth-floor mayor's office. The eleven-story building boasts a "green" roof on the city side filled with temperature-lowering green sod.

THE WATER TOWER

Left: The Chicago Water Tower stands at the corner of Michigan and Chicago avenues, having survived the devastation of the Great Fire of 1871. The castellated structure fashioned of yellow Lemont, Illinois, limestone was designed by architect William W. Boyington in 1869. Straight as an arrow—even after withstanding the scorching heat and fury of the fire—the building stands 154 feet tall and contains a standpipe 138 feet tall. Across the street is the pumping station formed of the same limestone. Originally built as a piece of modern urban plumbing, the survival of the Water Tower has given it a timeless and historic quality—a symbol of the city's own ability to press on after tragedy. Three-hundred Chicagoans perished in the fire; 90,000 were left homeless; and 17,450 buildings were destroyed. Cost estimates at the time totaled more than $200 million.

Right and below: The old Chicago Water Tower has gone on to give its name to the newer Water Tower Place, an urban development consisting of a high-end shopping mall and a seventy-four-story skyscraper. Though the old Water Tower is dwarfed by the enormity of its nearby neighbors—Skidmore, Owings, and Merrill's John Hancock Center; Loebl, Schlossman, and Hackl's Water Tower Place; and Lucien Lagrange's Park Hyatt Hotel and Residences—it still enjoys a unique Chicago celebrity. This is the heart of the Magnificent Mile. An evocative urban American architectural landscape has grown up here. Back in the 1920s, when Michigan Avenue was undergoing its first growth spurts as a commercial and social center of Chicago, the historic Water Tower was safely given its own parcel of protective geography which continues to keep it well guarded. It has become a significant tourist attraction and provides a continuous view of Chicago history, a reminder of the city's humble prairie roots and its remarkable ability to thrive.

ST. MICHAEL CHURCH

Left: There is an old saying in Chicago: "If you can hear the bells of St. Michael Church, you are in Old Town." St. Michael Church, located at 455 West Eugenie Street, in Old Town—the neighborhood bordered by Division Street on the south, Armitage Avenue on the north, Halsted Street on the west, and Clark Street on the east—was first settled in the 1850s by German Catholic immigrants, many from Bavaria, who established the church in 1852. The area had been home, first, to the Illinois, Miami, and Potawatomi peoples. This photo shows St. Michael following the Great Fire of 1871 when, miraculously, it became one of only six Chicago structures in the path of the inferno to semi-survive the blaze. It was the only building in Old Town to survive. Pre-fire pedigrees are rare in Chicago and add a unique patina of history to any object. The church had only been completed in 1869. Most of the city burned wildly because many structures were made out of wood. The sturdy red-brick exterior walls of the church must have been well made because enough of it remained intact for the building to be rebuilt in 1873. Fashioned in the Romanesque style by architect August Wallbaum, its seating capacity for 1,600 makes it cathedral-size.

Right: Today, both St. Michael Church, served by the Redemptorist Order of Priests, and the Old Town neighborhood are thriving. After becoming Chicago's great "hippie" neighborhood in the 1960s—a Haight-Ashbury–like community of artists, writers, and head-shop owners—the neighborhood enjoyed a great boom in real estate. Situated eight streets west of Lake Michigan's North Avenue Beach, Old Town (along the Wells Street corridor) is filled with gourmet shops and eateries. Nearby is the famed Second City comedy troupe that has been the testing ground for young comedians for more than fifty years. St. Michael Church refashioned its school into a condominium loft complex, which anchored some of the new growth in the neighborhood, no longer an ethnic German enclave. The neighborhood is one of the strictest communities for historic preservation of the clapboard, post-fire, vintage Victorian-designed homes. The church has been infused with a large population of young people that keeps the parochial life fresh and the weddings numerous. The tower of the church holds an illuminated four-sided steeple clock that can be seen for miles. Five great bells weighing one to three tons each still chime.

UNION STATION

Left: By the mid-nineteenth century, Chicago had become the center of American rail traffic. By 1860 the world's largest train station opened in Chicago in time for the city's first Republican National Presidential Convention. From then until the mid-twentieth century, the railroads were at the heart of Chicago commerce. Union Station was built at 225 South Canal Street between 1916 and 1925. It replaced the 1881 Union Station, itself a replacement of the 1874 Union Station built following the Great Fire of 1871. The station's interior is a massive eight-story, 100- by 269-foot space with a shimmering glass ceiling. Union Station's interior grandeur matches the exterior majesty of its Doric columns and travertine walls. The photo shows a panorama of the station and concourse across Canal Street from the terminal along the South Branch of the Chicago River. Refined engineering within this beaux arts–inspired terminus reflects the importance of America's national rail system. Nowhere was this more muscular or bold than in Chicago. At its height, more than 300 trains a day rolled into Chicago's Union Station.

Above: The old glamour and adventure of rail travel lives on in the architectural wonder of a neoclassical terminal like Union Station. The Concourse Building along the riverfront was razed in 1969 and in its place now sits a five-story Miesianlike black Cor-Ten steel structure housing the MidAmerica Commodity Exchange, with X-beams resembling those at the John Hancock Center. The structural design here includes a great cantilevered overhang above the commuter rail station for the suburban rail line station. With the Union Station itself, much of the internal operations of the head house, as the terminus is technically called, is belowground, complete with rail lines and track beds. Rail service has been consolidated over the decades under the national generic umbrella of Amtrak. Architect Lucien Lagrange undertook a large-scale renovation of Union Station back in 1992. Today the glamorous interior of the station is a favorite venue for events, with the vast waiting room transformed into a party space. Its elegance enhances any charity ball or high-end social. More than 50,000 people use the station each day during the commuter rush.

NAVY PIER

Left: Chicago's northern lakefront at the mouth of the Chicago River has always been the gateway to Chicago's massive urbanization. Since 1916 Navy Pier has been a part of that design. Originally known as Municipal Pier #2, it was a significant element of Daniel Burnham and Edward Bennett's 1909 *Plan of Chicago*. Pier #1 was never built further south. The pier itself is 3,330 feet long and sits on a fifty-acre landfill. In its early days, it was a fully functioning cargo facility and freight terminal fixed at the farthest eastern point of the city's urban center, adjacent to the mouth of the Chicago River. The advent of the mass-marketing of automobiles and trucks led to a serious decline in its functioning, and by the 1930s, the shipping business had greatly declined. But the pier was a highly social place to go as well, especially in hot weather when the breezes off the lake were the only air-conditioning around. A children's playground, dance hall, auditorium, and restaurants redirected the use of the pier. During World War II, the U.S. military made use of it for training 60,000 sailors and 15,000 pilots (including the forty-first president, George Herbert Walker Bush). In the postwar years, the University of Illinois's Chicago campus was located here until the construction of its vast urban campus on the West Side.

Above: Navy Pier has had an extraordinary rebirth that has made it Chicago's most popular tourist destination. The Streeterville neighborhood that abuts the area west of Lake Shore Drive has also undergone a renaissance. Already the ground has been prepared for the 150-story Chicago Spire, a Santiago Calatrava–designed high-rise that will be the tallest building in the United States. Since 1968, Navy Pier's neighbor has been the seventy-story shimmering glass and steel Lake Point Tower, once the home of Cubs slugger Sammy Sosa. It remains the only high-rise east of Lake Shore Drive. Alongside the pier today is Milton Lee Olive Park, a public lakefront park and the city's state-of-the-art Jardine Water Purification Plant that reconfigures the area. The pier today contains 50,000 square feet of exhibition space and 48,000 square feet of meeting room space. In addition, the refurbished pier hosts Chicago's only Ferris wheel, soaring to a height of 150 feet. The Chicago Shakespeare Theater Company resides there, near the IMAX theater and the carousel. This is home to a series of ships—the *Odyssey*, *Mystic Blue*, and others that cruise along the lakefront, together with water taxis and Chicago's tall ship, *Windy*.

NAVY PIER

Left: Chicago's Municipal Pier, designed by the noted architect Charles S. Frost, had been at the disposal of the U.S. military during World War II. It even resulted in its name change to Navy Pier. This photo displays the heavy utilitarian profile of a no-frills pier in 1947. With its training days behind it, and its lake freighter service all but ceased, Chicago officials found a fresh use for the massive structure. In 1946 the pier was transformed into the Chicago campus of the University of Illinois, accepting 3,730 students that first year—70 percent of them veterans with the passage of the G.I. Bill, which granted free university education to soldiers and sailors. The university took up 247,000 square feet of floor space. Though its main campus was 124 miles south of Chicago, the university would retain this lakeside campus until the mid-1960s when Mayor Richard J. Daley would level a large portion of the city's West Side as the permanent home for the university's new campus.

Right: Today, Navy Pier boasts a 50,000-square-foot Family Pavilion, seen here at the west end of the pier, which is anchored by Chicago Children's Museum. Three floors of hands-on learning make this a high-volume attraction. Playmaze, a baby-sized interactive city, is not to be missed. There is also a Climbing Schooner, a three-story replica of an 1850s sailing ship that children can climb. A carousel, Ferris wheel, swing ride called the Wave, and bounce ride called Light Tower make Navy Pier an all-day visit. In addition, there is an eighteen-hole miniature golf course. There is no better place in Chicago to ogle the skyline than the east end of Navy Pier. This is the farthest east you can get on dry land, and the panorama is expansive.

THE GOLD COAST

Left: In 1923 Chicago's Gold Coast had no competition when it came to swanky neighborhoods. The glamorous streetscapes were thick with exclusive town houses and co-ops designed by well-known Chicago architects for the families of wealthy industrialists, trust fund tycoons, and socialites. This small landscape ran along the shoreline of Lake Michigan, south of Lincoln Park to Chicago Avenue, and from LaSalle Street to Lake Shore Drive. Many of those who occupied the vintage luxury homes and "in-town" apartments had country homes as well. Grocery stores and markets were filled with the domestic staffs of local residents shopping and picking up necessities. Hotel king Potter Palmer started it all by building his wife a Rhine Castle in 1890 along the curve of Lake Shore Drive. These were the Chicagoans who never needed to go south of the river; some prided themselves that they "never went south of Saks" (Fifth Avenue). East Lake Shore Drive, Astor Street, North State Parkway, and Burton Place were home to people like Edith Rockefeller McCormick, Robert Todd Lincoln, Joseph Medill McCormick, and Nancy Davis Reagan.

Above: The Gold Coast is still Chicago's most exclusive neighborhood. The social etiquette of the past may not be as strong and the trust funds may be a little more sparse, but there is no more socially conscious address than Lake Shore Drive and its surroundings. Many of the more lavish mansions have disappeared, and residents are more egalitarian, relying far less on domestic help. CEOs now occupy the elegant domestic dwellings once fashioned for the barons of industry. The neighborhood is stuffed with great architectural designs, such as the James Charnley House on Astor Street, designed in 1892 by Frank Lloyd Wright, Sanford White's domestic palace, designed for newspaper heiress Elinor Patterson's wedding to Cyrus McCormick, the namesake grandson of the inventor of the reaper. The Gold Coast has been home to Hugh Hefner, as well as Oprah Winfrey and the cardinal archbishop of Chicago.

LAKEFRONT

Chicagoans take the splendor of the lakefront for granted, especially the grandeur of the near north esplanade. Most never realize that this is all man-made. Lake Michigan is not a tidal ocean, and fresh sand is not an ongoing eco-commodity. This photograph below looks as if a great ocean liner or a Great Lake's freighter has run aground. But this is just the North Avenue Beach House—a watering hole throughout the summer, complete with burgers, beer, and sun. It is a crowded favorite to meet friends along the beach where everything from volleyball and badminton can be found. The waters of Lake Michigan are crystal clear and warm in summer. Beaches are easy to get to and public transportation is plentiful. Underpasses and overpasses make beach access easy. But few ever recognize that this splendor was shaped by the hand of man, manicured and refashioned to fit the tastes and needs of beachgoing Chicagoans.

LINCOLN PARK

Left: Lincoln Park, seen here in 1936, is Chicago's largest—a 1,200-acre site named for Abraham Lincoln. It runs from North Avenue (1600 North) on the southern end, to Foster Avenue (5200 North) on the northern rim, along the shoreline of Lake Michigan. Before it was designated a public park, it contained the city's cemeteries. Plans were made in 1864 to form a waterfront park and move the cemeteries to the farther reaches of the city. After President Lincoln's death, the city decided to name it in his honor. By the time the Chicago Fire spread across the city, many graves had already been moved.

Above: The rolling playing fields and elegant public statues honoring such notables as René-Robert Cavelier, Sieur de La Salle (the first European to see the Chicago area when it was still part of New France), William Shakespeare, Goethe, Friedrich Schiller, Alexander Hamilton, and Sir Georg Solti fill the parkland setting here. An expanded zoological park also includes a children's farm zoo. The old bridle paths were deeded to the people of Chicago by the Marshall Field family and are now used as jogging paths. The Lincoln Park Conservatory is a botanical wonder. The park setting includes marinas and a golf course, as well as a summer theater and an abundance of entertainment throughout the year. Today the park is edged by a long line of residential high-rises, Chicago's Upper East Side, with good restaurants and countless chic shops. The lakefront beach here became Chicago's very first public beach in 1895.

IRVING PARK

Left: This photo is focused on the heartland of the East Lakeview neighborhood and shows Immaculata High School along Irving Park Road, where Lake Shore Drive curves inland (top right). Designed in 1922 by Frank Lloyd Wright's apprentice, the noted Prairie School architect Barry Byrne, the high school's modern design was shaped perfectly for its environmentally significant placement. Independent Lakeview Township incorporated into Chicago in 1889, but it had been settled by the area's first European, Conrad Sulzer, back in 1837, the same year Chicago incorporated as a city. Irving Park Road was named for the famed writer Washington Irving, author of *The Legend of Sleepy Hollow*. The public golf course along Lake Shore Drive was established in 1932 and remains one of Chicago's finest. The neighborhood was first settled by German and Swedish immigrants, though this had been the home of the Ottawa, Miami, and Winnebago peoples.

Above: Today, social and cultural expansion makes the Lakeview neighborhood a desirable place to live. Now obscured by taller buildings, Immaculata High School is currently the home of the American Islamic College, still beautiful in the contours of Prairie design. The streetscapes of Lakeview along Broadway, Halsted, Sheffield, Southport, and Lake Shore Drive are manicured and refined. Fashionable shoreline high-rises share the atmosphere created by finely remodeled single-family homes and vintage apartment buildings. Nearby Halsted Street, south of Addison Street, is home to America's largest gay and lesbian community, and Wrigley Field is not far away. Waveland Golf Course is now known as the Sydney R. Marovitz Golf Course, and nearby Montrose Harbor to the north and Belmont Harbor to the south are filled with sailboats and large motor launches in the summer.

BIOGRAPH THEATER

Left: The Biograph Theater, at 2433 North Lincoln Avenue, was designed by architect Samuel N. Crowen and built in 1914. From the beginning, it was one of Chicago's most distinguished neighborhood movie houses, a business that was just starting to emerge before World War I. Lincoln Avenue was not far away from the center of American filmmaking in Chicago. Two large studios (Selig and Essanay) called Chicago home before California. But no element of Hollywood could compare with the unfolding of real life here. On the night of July 22, 1934, America's most-wanted criminal—the infamous bank robber John Dillinger—was lured to the Biograph by girlfriend Polly Hamilton. At 10:30 p.m., Dillinger walked out of the theater and was quickly confronted by federal agents. Running into a nearby alley, Dillinger began a shoot-out with the agents who returned five rounds of bullets, three of which hit Dillinger. He died in nearby Alexian Brothers Hospital. Dillinger's betrayer became known as "the lady in red"—although her dress was orange it appeared red under the theater's lights. This photo is from July 24, 1934, two days after Dillinger was gunned down.

Above and right: Today the legend of Dillinger is not far away from the historic Biograph Theater, although it is now known as the Victory Gardens Theater at the Biograph. (Victory Gardens is a company well known within the Chicago community.) Live theatrical productions are mainly shown at this historic location. In 2007 the character of Dillinger, played by Johnny Depp, walked Lincoln Avenue once more when the entire streetscape was altered to its former 1934 profile for use in the film *Public Enemy*. Situated in Chicago's Lincoln Park neighborhood, the theater is surrounded by the expanded urban campus of DePaul University.

WRIGLEY FIELD

Above: Since 1916 the Chicago Cubs have played baseball in what is arguably the sport's best home, Wrigley Field—a sacred space for many Chicagoans. Built in 1914, it was known as Weeghman Park for the Chicago Federal League, but became known as Cubs Park between 1920 and 1926, renamed for America's chewing gum king, William Wrigley Jr. The ballpark is located at the corner of Addison and Clark streets, and though the official name of the neighborhood nearby is Lakeview, to Chicagoans this is really Wrigleyville. Only Boston's Fenway Park (1912) can boast an older Major League ballpark pedigree. "Mr. Cub"—Ernie Banks, one of the Cubs most revered former players—renamed the park the "Friendly Confines" long ago. Perhaps Wrigley Field's most outstanding characteristic is its ivy-covered outfield walls that change color and texture throughout the baseball season. Though the Chicago Cubs have not been in a World Series since 1945, Wrigley Field still attracts some of the largest crowds in baseball. Cubs fans are true and loyal, demonstrating a sense of cohesion that outshines many teams. They achieved a Division Championship in 2008—but as all Chicagoans know, "there is always next year."

Few things stay the same in Chicago, but loyalty to the Cubs is one. Fans today cheer on with spirit and hope. And Wrigley Field is fresher than it was when it opened in 1914. Since 1981 the team was owned by the Tribune Company and only sold in a deal approved in 2009. And in what was one of the most dramatic moments in Cubs history, August 8, 1988, the very first "night game" was played, ending an unbroken tradition of day games that had lasted for ninety-one years. Because Lake Michigan is less than eight blocks from Wrigley Field, the winds off the lake "blow in" and make it difficult for players to hit home runs during the early spring. In the summer when the winds change direction and come from the warm southwest, they have the opposite effect, helping to "blow out" a home run when you least expect it. The neighborhood around Wrigley Field has been gentrified and boasts one of the largest post-college populations in Chicago. Many surrounding three-flat apartment buildings have bumped out their roof decks in recent years so that they can host large groups who can view the action on the field from across the street.

EDGEWATER BEACH HOTEL

Left: The imposing Edgewater Beach Hotel (top right) was built along the north lakefront in 1916 in the Edgewater neighborhood near Berwyn Avenue, between Sheridan Road and Lake Shore Drive. This was an important social site beyond the contours of downtown Chicago that gave the lakefront a sparkling patina of elegance. The hotel offered a private beach and seaplane service for its guests, who included presidents Franklin D. Roosevelt and Dwight Eisenhower, Marilyn Monroe, Frank Sinatra, and Judy Garland. Celebrities and regular guests came for the entertainment in the 1930s and 1940s—the big band era—including Xavier Cugat, Wayne King, Glenn Miller, Tommy Dorsey, and Benny Goodman. This photograph was taken in 1923.

Above: In 1928 the Edgewater Beach Apartments were built with the same pink Art Deco architecture as the main hotel. The hotel was cut off from the beach when the extension of Lake Shore Drive was completed in 1954. After years of decline, the hotel was closed and razed in 1967, though the apartments remain. Many vintage buildings from the 1920s and 1930s still dot a streetscape that is rich with churches and synagogues. Amid the greenery of the lakeshore parkland is the Saddle and Cycle Club, a private bastion of old money to which members long ago could ride their horses from downtown on the bridle paths along the lake. In the distance, the Loyola University campus sits by the water's edge, and beyond that, the campus of Northwestern University in Evanston.

Since 1851 Northwestern University has sat beside the waters of Lake Michigan in Evanston, the leafy suburb that is Chicago's immediate neighbor to the north. School founder John Evans gave his name to the town in 1857, when he struggled to create a collegiate academic institution to serve the people of the Northwest Territory. The nine original founders were all Methodists, but they stressed the "non-sectarian" character to the school. Northwestern was a founding member in 1895 of the Big Ten Conference of Midwestern collegiate athletics. The university, shown here in 1907, sits on 240 acres of rolling lakefront property. University Hall, the castellated towered building at the upper left of this photo, is the university's oldest building still standing on campus. Northwestern has gone on to distinguish itself as an academic institution of extraordinary quality that ranks with Ivy League schools.

NORTHWESTERN UNIVERSITY

In this contemporary photo, the university looks more like a midsize American town. The footprint of the campus was greatly expanded from 1962 to 1964 when two million cubic yards of sand were hauled from nearby Indiana steel mills to create a landfill that moved the campus nearly a quarter-mile out into the waters of the lake. The architectural firm of Skidmore, Owings, and Merrill directed the project that cost $6.5 million. United Nations Ambassador Adlai Stevenson, a 1926 Law School grad, was the keynote when the expanded campus opened. Ten more acres were added in 1968. The strategic plan for this expansion allowed the university to move east, rather than west into Evanston proper. In the foreground, at the right, is Pick-Staiger Concert Hall; to its left is the Block Museum of Art and the three pods of the four-million-volume

university library (1970) by architect Walter Netsch; and the 1899 red-brick Fisk Hall, is at the lower center of the frame, by architect Daniel Burnham. All present a variety of contrasting architectural styles. At the lower right is the tip of Centennial Park and the spacious beach that begins there. In the far distance at the top, the bleached-white, ninety-foot dome of the Baha'i House of Worship in neighboring Wilmette, a 138-foot tall Persian-inspired religious center rises above the trees. The academic achievements of Northwestern are known the world over and its physical expansion across the original land and throughout Evanston itself is a mark of that achievement. The Kellogg School of Management and the Medill School of Journalism have international reputations.

MAP OF CHICAGO

CHICAGO · · IN 1868

CHICAGO IN 1820.

from Schiller Street North Side to 12th Street South Side.

The city extends beyond the section line of 12th street given here yet a distance of 3 miles to Egan Avenue (City Limits) on the South Side and a distance of 1¼ mile beyond Schiller St. to Fullerton Avenue on the North Side.

The entire length of the city from North to South being 7 Miles and breadth from East to West 3½ Miles.